MY FUTURE MY FINANCE

5 Stages towards a protected

monetary eventual fate of your loved ones

Copyright

Copyright © 2022 by Robert Napoleon
Protected by copyright law. No piece of this distribution might be imitated, put away or communicated in any structure or using any and all means, electronic, mechanical, copying, recording, examining, or in any case without composed authorization from the distributor.

It is against the law to duplicate this book, present it on a site, or circulate it by some other means without consent.

Robert Napoleon states the ethical right to be distinguished as the author of this work.

FIRST EDITION

Robert Napoleon2

Table of Contents

Introduction

Chapter One: Personal Banking
- The 5 Most Important Financial Lessons for Teenagers.

Chapter Two: Good Financial Management
- Individual financial management
- The significance of good financial management in life.

Chapter Three: Personal Finance

Chapter Four: How to Make Effective Investments in Our Children's Futures
- Finance Our Children's Future.
- Savings Plan for Your Child, Invest in Your Child's Future.
- How to Invest.
- Budgeting for Education for Your Child As parents, we must all be extremely realistic.
- Financing our Children's Future Other Than Education.

Chapter Five: Parental Financial Habits That Affect A Child's Future Financial Situation .
- How to Teach Your Child Good Financial Habits
- Bad Money Habits to Avoid

About The Author

Introduction

This book exposes the simple secrets and tips on how one can be financially buoyant in order to care for our loved ones and help them to secure a future void of scarcity, wants, necessity and lots more.

It also reflects on the importance of the necessity to save, discovering new ways on how one can invest to secure a greater future.

The ability to manage our finances is the secret to being financially stable and buoyant. This book entails more ways and secrets to successfully carry this task out.

Robert Napoleon4

CHAPTER ONE

Personal Banking

However, building a solid financial foundation early on is more important than ever as young adults face increasing levels of credit card debt and student loan debt.

Consider teaching teens age-appropriate money habits that can last a lifetime by learning how teens tend to spend and save.

The 5 Most Important Financial Lessons for Teenagers.

Parents who have teenagers know that money management is not easy.

- Know where the money comes from.
  While some parents directly pay for things or give their teens allowances, others work for themselves.

- Be aware of the advantages of saving money.
  The majority of teenagers save money, and by saving a small amount each month, they can save a lot in the long run.

Saving $25 per month Saving $50 per month One year $300 $600 Five years $1,500 $3,000 Ten years $3,000 $6,000 Inflation and account interest are not taken into account by the numbers.

- Keep track of expenses to stay within your budget. In 2020, the typical teen spent $2,150 on food, clothing, and entertainment.

- Establish good credit, prevent future debt accumulation, and educate your teen about the risks and responsibilities associated with credit card use.

The average amount of credit card debt that Americans have by the age of 20 is $2,319, according to sources: Experian, CreditCards.com, and Think long-term Thinking about the future can teach teens to better achieve their own goals and help them start saving for themselves.

- What teens think 35% believe they will have $100,000 saved by the time they are 30. 43% plan to pay off student loans by the time they are 30. 66% believe they will own a home by the time they are 30.

CHAPTER TWO

Good Financial Management

The Importance Of Good Financial Management in Life
Financial management is an important part of our day-to-day lives.

We get so caught up in our day-to-day lives that we forget how important financial management is.

It is impossible to live a life of servitude and know how to pay your bills and get out of financial debt without understanding how to manage your money.

Your money will be well managed if you have the necessary financial management skills.

Individual financial management

Individual financial management is the topic of this section. It includes how you control your spending and investments as well as your savings.

Banking, budgeting, insurance, retirement planning, and other aspects of financial management are among the general categories.

The significance of good financial management in life.

Financial management entails achieving both short-term and long-term financial objectives. The importance of financial management cannot be overstated, but here are just a few.

- **Helps you manage your budget, savings, and expenses, as well as your financial needs.**

Personal finance ensures financial security, increases your assets and increases your standard of living ensures that one's financial requirements are met. Money is the most important thing for any person.

One aspect is making money, and another is making sure your needs are met with the money.

Important aspects of ensuring that financial requirements are met include having a plan that specifies an individual's income, expenses, spending strategies, and goals for the future.

If the following factors are managed effectively, financial management ensures that an individual meets their financial obligations.

Keeping to a monthly budget, paying bills on time, managing loans, saving for retirement, managing credit cards, and tracking credit score are all advantages of having good personal finance and money management skills. You can also take advantage of opportunities, work on responsibilities, and face financial challenges.

- **Helps you keep track of your money.**

If you don't have a plan for your money, you'll either spend more money than you make or buy things you don't need. You can effectively

Robert Napoleon8

manage your income if you have a sound plan for managing your finances.

You will only spend what is absolutely necessary, save money for the future, and invest appropriately if you have a sound financial plan.

Knowing which expenses to handle first and which later is helpful with financial management. You will effectively pay your taxes, invest, and pay your bills each month.

- **Savings, expenses, and a budget**

  You'll end up in a lot of debt if you spend your money on things you don't need or if you spend it on your whims and fancy. This could happen if you spend more than you need to, which could cause your finances to become unstable.

Budgeting your income is made easier when you manage your finances. Planning your income with a budget helps you decide where to spend your money, how much to save, and how much to invest.

Follow your lifestyle plan, stick to your budget, don't spend too much, and put your money toward savings. You can get through difficult times with the money you save and invest.

Look here: How can a budget be created and defined?

- **Personal Finance**

  Managing your money can be made easier with personal finance. You can keep track of your spending habits and expenses with financial management help. It makes it simple to increase your cash flow.

The following are some strategies for improving cash flow.

Planning your taxes, spending wisely, and keeping a proper budget will ensure that your money is not wasted. Because it ensures that you are on the right financial course, having a personal financial plan is very important.

- **Financial Security**

   Financial management ensures your family's financial security. Financial freedom is achieved through effective financial management. Financial security is provided by financial freedom.

You and your family will have financial security if you have the right savings, insurance, and investment strategy in place.

Gain a better understanding of your finances and increase your assets to increase your assets. You are in a good financial position when you own assets. Sometimes liabilities are linked to assets. Your net worth will rise if you determine the value of your assets.

Your assets will grow with your financial management. You will be financially secure if you settle your liabilities by paying off your debts and investing more in fixed assets. By effectively managing your finances, you can grow your assets in this manner.

Robert Napoleon10

- Your standard of living will rise as a result of better financial management. Your net worth will rise more rapidly the more you plan for your savings. Your savings will increase the more you plan for your finances. Saving money can help you overcome financial obstacles. Your standard of living will rise as a result of having good financial management.

In conclusion, the first step in financial management is to comprehend your finances. You will experience a severe financial crisis if you do not implement effective financial management. Ensure that your financial management is so efficient that it safeguards your future.

Robert Napoleon11

CHAPTER THREE

Personal Finance

A step-by-step guide to creating a personal financial plan
When it comes to your finances and plans, it can be challenging to strike a balance between short-term desires, long-term goals, and unforeseen occurrences that are beyond your control.

It can be difficult to figure out how to pay bills while also planning for the future, whether you need groceries, want to retire, or need your car fixed.

This series of tutorials can be of assistance.It walks you through everything you need to know to make a personal financial plan and get your finances in order step by step. It is acceptable if some of these steps have already been taken. It's fine if you haven't yet. Start with just one task and work your way up or you could just tackle the whole thing on a rainy, long weekend with a big pot of coffee and a dog by your feet.)

Let's get going.

- **Set financial objectives.**

It's always a good idea to know precisely why you're saving money.

- **Establish a budget.**

Take this as your monthly plan for savings and investing as well as cash flow. With our budgeting worksheet, plan for taxes, you can give yourself permission to decide where and how to send your money.

- **Create an emergency fund.**

This can help you keep more of your money for next year.

If life throws you a curveball and you aren't prepared financially, all of your planning won't help. An emergency fund can come in handy in this situation.

- **Control debt.**

A crucial component of developing a financial plan is comprehending and managing debt.

- **Insurance provides protection.**

Life can alter in a split second. A sound financial strategy anticipates the unanticipated while hoping for the best. Insurance facilitates this.

- **Make a retirement plan.**

Think about what you want your money to do for you when you retire, even if it's a long way off, and make a plan to get there.

- **Invest beyond your 401(k).**

Put an engine behind your savings strategy to achieve your mid- and long-term objectives. This is what investing can accomplish.

- **Plan your estate.**

An estate plan, which also specifies who will make decisions regarding your finances and health care if you

Robert Napoleon13

are unable to do so for yourself, is not necessary for anyone who is rich, old, married, or a parent.

Robert Napoleon14

CHAPTER FOUR

How to Make Effective Investments in Our Children's Futures

As parents, we should make investing in our children's futures an important part of our overall investment strategy over time. How we invest has a significant impact on the financial future of your children. Everything in regards to financing their future is included: from taking care of them to paying for their daily needs; Furthermore, sending children to school is one of the most expensive aspects of raising children, so the earlier we begin investing, the better. We are advised to begin this trend before having children if at all possible, even as young adults.

Finance Our Children's Future

It is advantageous to begin saving early for a child's education. As a young adult, begin to put things away; because investing's compound interest effect has a significant impact.

Savings Plan for Your Child, Invest in Your Child's Future.

At a minimum, parents should put at least 20 percent of their income into a long-term savings plan that lets your money earn interest; Therefore, when you look back in ten to fifteen years, you will have a sizable sum of money not only for the expenses of the family but also for the child's education. When you focus on this, it will become a way of life, and you will tend to invest in yourself first before buying things.

How to Invest
 Here, the whole idea of diversification comes into play. Parents are encouraged to conduct research on the internet or to locate a reputable investment professional with whom they can consult for initial advice regarding the best investments. It will be difficult to decide which investments to make if you have no idea what you want to accomplish. How can I invest? encompasses the entire idea of diversification; due to the fact that a particular instrument's interest rates vary from one to the next;such as investing in real estate or stocks, which are returns-oriented investments.

A lot of research is required when investing in your child's education in particular. At the secondary school and university levels, education typically comes at a high price; Parents are open to sending their children abroad for higher education at the university level. Early on in a child's life, parents should have an idea of what they want;the kind of school they want their child to go to, as well as the number of years. They can use this information to investigate the number of fees and taxes as well as the investments they could make in the long run to achieve this goal. Such matters can be resolved by presenting them to an expert in investments.

Budgeting for Education for Your Child As parents, we must all be extremely realistic.

Putting yourself under such pressure because you want to pay for your children's education is not in your family's best interest. You don't have to spend a lot of time researching to find a good school that fits your budget;to the point where you are not jeopardizing your health or your plans for a future retirement. What happens when the children graduate if you risk everything to send them to an expensive school? As they mature into responsible adults, they will also need to take care of themselves. It's time for parents to stop thinking that their children are their retirement plan; Therefore, we must approach it in that manner and determine what we can afford.

Parents can find online learning plans to supplement what the school does not offer their child. The ability to code and artificial intelligence, for instance, are the future; Even if your children aren't in school, you can start teaching them how to code with fantastic plans that are often free or only a fraction of the cost. Parents must be able to work backwards and identify what their children need to succeed in the present and the future. Education is a big expense, but it should be spent wisely.

Robert Napoleon17

Financing our Children's Future Other Than Education.

One of the most important things parents should plan for is healthcare. A good health insurance plan is necessary for children to have good health; This must be viewed by parents as an investment in their children's future. Their fundamental requirements are another crucial aspect; Parents must also make plans for the family's basic needs, which can consume up to 50% of the family's income.

- Opening bank accounts for your kids is a good way to help them pay for their future;because it provides them with early financial literacy instruction.They are able to comprehend what it means to have an account by having a bank account opened for them.
- Get them started on investing and familiarize them with concepts like the stock market;They are not excessively young.Ask them about these conversations to see how interested they are;Let them investigate the things they want to invest in.

Even as young adults without children, we are all encouraged to plan for our children's futures and make them the best they can be.

Robert Napoleon18

CHAPTER FIVE

Parental Financial Habits That Affect A Child's Future Financial Situation .

Parental influence is the most potent for any child. They acquire and gradually acquire their parents' habits. When they are young, they naturally look up to and want to be like their parents. This is evident in their conduct. They pick up nonverbal and verbal cues that could also have an impact on their behavior and future. The financial routines are the same. Parents shape children's views on money and influence their spending and saving habits. The most common disconnect or mistake that occurs in every middle-class family is that parents frequently do not realize that their bad financial habits can have an impact on their children, which is why they pass on those bad financial habits to their children.

Being a parent necessitates an understanding of your habits, which can have an impact on your children's financial future.

How to Teach Your Child Good Financial Habits

- Talking About Money Families should talk about money with their children.

  Discuss with your child the spending, saving, and financial planning for the future of the family's finances.This way, they can learn how important money is and build a financial foundation for themselves as they get older.

This is very important because, if they don't realize how important money is, they will start spending it without thinking, which will ruin their financial future.

- **Being Organized**

The best way to organize your finances is to create a budget and stick to it.Create a budget and compare your monthly inflows and outflows to avoid missing payments for bills and other obligations.The capacity to manage and monitor your finances in all of these waysConsider that if you do all of these things, your child will also learn the same things, ensuring a prosperous financial future.However, if you fail to do so, your child will gradually observe all of these characteristics in you.They won't mind if you don't stick to a budget and pay your bills on time, and they will do the same when they get older.

- **The only way to achieve your financial objectives is to plan for savings and investments.**

Additionally, establishing a goal and selecting the appropriate tools to help you achieve it are both essential. Money is in the same boat. It's critical to set financial objectives. You won't have to worry about your money or your mind if you buy a house or a costly gadget in a planned way.

In the same way, you can't expect a fixed deposit to work for 15 years if you keep your money there. However, when it reaches maturity, 15 years from now, it will return to you.

When children grow up, they are more likely to do the same for their family if their parents carefully plan their finances and have savings and investments in place.

The most crucial emergency savings account is this one. You have no idea how much it will cost you and emergencies can occur at any time without notice.

What's more important is what happens if you don't have enough at the time? As a result, you should prepare for it and contribute a portion of your monthly income to your emergency fund. If you do this, you will never experience a financial crisis. Additionally, you will instill in your child a healthy financial habit. They will definitely incorporate this into their financial practices as they attempt to follow in their parents' footsteps.

Bad Money Habits to Avoid

- **Overspending and Living Without a Budget.**

Parents who do not discuss the household budget with their children and who do not even create a budget typically have spoiled children. Toys are the first item on a child's wish list, followed by gadgets over time. Even things they don't need are demanded of them. They are completely unaware of the significance of a budget and money. When they get older, they will apply the same principles to their lives.

The majority of us only have so much money, so spending decisions should be based on family priorities if you want your child to have a better financial future. Give only what your child absolutely needs, even if you can afford to buy them.

- **Arguments About Money**

A lot of people argue about money. However, doing this in front of your children is detrimental to their future. Never engage in money-related argumentation in front of children, and never attempt to do so.

They become accustomed to such situations when they see them, and it becomes acceptable for them to argue with other people about money or anything else. Even when they are young, they will start arguing about their pocket money.

- **Living Life to the Fullest Everyone wants their child's dreams to come true.**

Yet, this doesn't imply that you ought to satisfy every one of their requests from adolescence itself. They will believe that you have so much money that you can buy and provide them with everything they desire if you start meeting their demands. Because of this, their demands will continue to rise as they get older, eventually leading to them being spoiled. Additionally, it will negatively impact their future. Therefore, don't be a king and hesitate before complying with your children's demands.

- **Taking on Debts.**

Parents who have a number of debts, either because they don't know how to manage their money well or because they need to, like paying off their credit card bills in full, won't be able to keep a budget, balance their income and expenses, or even save enough money to reach their goals.

Children may even be left to lend themselves in the event of a sudden parent's death. They are demonstrating to the children that it is more important to live within one's means now than in the future and teaching them not to live below one's means.

Children learn from everything they see in their daily lives because they are the blank canvas. They don't have to grow up in a wealthy family to learn how to manage money well; all they need is a good example to follow.

Robert Napoleon23

ABOUT THE AUTHOR

Robert Napoleon is Keen on the interest of teens, parents and students on how one can be financially buoyant in order to be able to secure finance for the future.
He's more than willing to help others in self development.

Robert Napoleon24

www.ingramcontent.com/pod-product-compliance
Lightning Source LLC
Chambersburg PA
CBHW050329220526
45465CB00005B/2203